A DOG SIZE HOLE IN YOUR HEART

By

Russ Lawson

Dealing with the loss of a furry family member

Dedication: To my wife, Melody, of almost 55 years. We have literally been around the world in our lives and our fur babies have been an intricate part of that life. However it all began because she first saw a puppy and said, "If I ever had a puppy, I want one like that!" That changed our lives and our world.

Copyright 2021

Index

Introduction

God obviously had a reason for creating dogs, we can't be sure just what that reason is, but perhaps one day we will get the opportunity to ask him. Whatever the reason there can be no doubt that they find their way into our hearts. There is no doubt in my mind that they become a real part of our emotional family and at times are planted just as deeply in our hearts as our physical children. We adopt them, learn to love them, play with them, raise them, train them in the proper way to act and care for them, but the very sad truth is that we eventually will lose them to death. We understand that they have shorter life spans than do we, but we choose to love them anyway and when they pass it truly does leave a dog sized hole in our heart.

Somewhere along the line of time dogs have earned the title of "Mans Best Friend. I'm sure there may be some who would take exception to that, (perhaps another animal relation has been closer for them), but for me and my wife we found it to be true.

I always liked this little story below, though it doesn't deal strictly with dogs, it does deal with sacrifice. I have no idea where it originated, but it has been around the Internet and Facebook many times for many years.

On the first day God created the dog. God said, "Sit all day by the door of your house and bark at

anyone who comes in or walks past. I will give you a life span of twenty years." The dog said, "That's too long to be barking. Give me ten years and I'll give you back the other ten."

So God agreed.

On the second day God created the monkey. God said, "Entertain people, do monkey tricks and make them laugh. I'll give you a twenty-year life span." The monkey said, "Monkey tricks for twenty years? I don't think so. Dog gave you back ten, so that's what I'll do too, okay?"

And God agreed.

On the third day God created the cow. "You must go to the field with the farmer all day long and suffer under the sun, have calves, and give milk to support the farmer. I will give you a life span of sixty years."

The cow said, "That's kind of a tough life you want me to live for sixty years. Let me have twenty and I'll give back the other forty."

And God agreed again.

On the fourth day God created man. God said, "Eat, sleep, play, marry and enjoy your life. I'll give you twenty years."

Man said, "What? Only twenty years? Tell you what, I'll take my twenty, and the forty the cow gave back, and the ten the monkey gave back, and the ten the dog gave back, that makes eighty, okay?"

Okay," said God, "You've got a deal."

So that is why the first twenty years we eat, sleep, play, and enjoy ourselves; the next forty years we slave in the sun to support our family; the next ten years we do monkey tricks to entertain the grandchildren; and the last ten years we sit on the front porch and bark at everyone.

Life has now been explained to you.

....

OK, that may not really explain life, but it does deal with the idea of sacrifice that dogs seem willing to make for us humans. If you want to understand love, loyalty or faithfulness, then look at a dog's life. Look at how they seem to give all of those things when many times their humans often don't deserve it. That's why we love dogs; that is why many of us can't imagine a life without having a dog in it.

My purpose in writing this is just to take a short look at what dogs have meant to our many friends and my wife and I. You will find inside, the hearts joys and hurts of some who have shared their stories and see how we all dealt with it when death takes them. I want to take a look at how we deal with the dog sized hole that is left in our hearts when they are no longer with us.

HOW TO BEGIN…

Knowing where to begin is always difficult, especially when dealing with difficult subjects such as the death of a furry family member.

Where do you begin to deal with this deep pain you experience except at the beginning and try to understand the relationship?

To be honest the only way you can truly understand what it is like to lose a pet to death is to have lost one yourself. My wife and I have had the terrible reality of losing three pets, two we had to make the decision to have put to sleep to end their pain, the other to a sudden illness.

The pain of those deaths were just as heart rending as when we lose a human member of our family. Yes, we realize there is a difference between humans and animals, but try telling that to your heart when you hold the lifeless body of a companion who had been an intimate part of your life for years. Friends and family try to reason with you and comfort you, by telling you that they were only an animal, but in truth, they were much more than that to us! Those of us who have adopted those furry children understand that, though those who have not probably won't understand the depth of that relationship of having a "fur baby".

Ching our first fur baby

OUR PERSONAL JOURNEY

Our journey with a furry family member began with a visit to a friend's home. As we sat on the front porch visiting a neighbor came by with a little ball of fur that was so cute we just had to ask about it. We found out it was a Peek-a-poo and my wife said, "If I ever decide I want a dog, that's what I want." The problem is that you couldn't find those mixed breeds very easily at that time (now they have become designer dogs and much more expensive). But, loving my wife as I do, and knowing she had a birthday coming up before long, I began to search for a breeder that sold Peek-a-poo's. It took a month or so, but I did locate someone about 30 miles from our home, we made arrangements to go and see the puppies at once.

We arrived at a nice home in the country and were ushered into a lovely home and they brought out a couple of the pups. My wife fell in love with the runt of the litter who pranced around so cute. Needless to say we left with a new furry child. We were new at having a pet so the first thing we decided to do was go straight to the vet's office just to have her checked out and get her shots. She checked out just fine and before we got her home Ty-Qui-Ching, Ching for short, (the name we chose), became part of our family.

Interestingly enough we just happened to be reading the newspaper later in the week and saw where the local pet protection group had just raided the house where we purchased Ching, and it turned out to be a Puppy Mill. We were completely unaware of this at the time, so we always felt that we rescued her. It didn't take long for us to fall in love with her and she reciprocated, I was her "papa" and my wife was "mama" from then on.

Her first night with us we put her in a box in the laundry room with a clock and a stuffed toy… and she cried… so we moved the box into the bedroom with us… and she cried. So shortly after that she ended up on the end of our bed and she slept there for 16 years and never caused one problem.

Ching was so smart that in a matter of days she understood she needed to go outside to go to the bathroom. She also she understood English better than some young children and learned tricks in record time. She would respond to almost anything you would ask her or tell her to do. I came to understand that in a couple of years she understood well over 100 words and could understand many sentences as we talked to her. To say the least she was our baby and our furry child and became firmly embedded in our hearts.

She loved to take rides and look out the window. One time I told her, "Tell me where to turn when I get to our road". I never expected it, but when we got to the turn she looked at me a barked. She did so many tricks and responded so well that I made it a regular practice to take her Nursing homes, extended care centers and even day care schools and put on little performances. She seemed to love it and of course everyone else did also.

Ching was part of our family in every way; both of our sons had their Senior High School pictures taken with her in the pictures. And, in 1990 when we moved to Kenya East Africa we made part of the agreement that she went with us. We eventually came back to the states and she of course was with us every step of the way.

After we had been back a few years we embarked upon the adventure of building our own house, not hiring it done, but actually doing the physical work ourselves. I had been raised as a carpenter, my father being a general contractor, so we had the skills necessary. Of course it helped that my father was able to come over and act as foreman on the job and help us with so many things.

However during that period of time Ching's health began to fail. She lost part of her sight and began loosing control of her bladder and she would get lost in a room and couldn't find her way out as if she had dementia, she was having more and more trouble getting around as her joints hurt.

The hardest thing we ever had to do!

We tried our best to deal with it, but eventually the Vet said it was time to let her go. We struggled with the decision for a couple of weeks, but finally chose to ease her suffering. That was the hardest thing we ever had to do and we had been through some difficult times in our lives. I held this little bundle of trusting love in my arms as the Vet gave her the shot and I held her until she breathed the last. My wife and I cried our eyes out, we called our youngest son who came home from work and he cried with us and we buried her in our yard in the country under a lilac bush with her favorite toy.

We were heart broken, for a long time we looked for her often, expecting to see her following us or telling us it was time for her canned food or time to go to bed. She was our furry child, our baby for 16 years, part of our family and part of our heart and when she died it left a terrible, dog sized hole in our hearts. Not only that, but at times, no matter how you tried to rationalize it, even if the Vet said it was time, we felt like we had killed her rather than giving her release from her aging body and it hurt and at times still hurts.

LOOSING A PET IS NEVER EASY!

About the time Ching died my sister's little dog died also. Levi went to sleep one evening and never woke up in the morning. Levi wasn't exactly a rescue dog, but he came from a troubled life. When they first adopted him he was afraid of everything and spent much of his time hiding under the bed. It took a long time before they earned his trust and then for the longest time he would still hide when strangers came to visit. They also felt that at some time he may have been left out in the cold and gotten frostbite. He hated to go out in the cold and acted like it hurt his feet. They did a wonderful job of giving him a home and he became one of their kids for many years. I wrote the following piece as a Newspaper article for a column I wrote at the time.

HEY GOD! HOW DO YOU LIKE YOUR NEW DOG?

Death surrounds us in this world as do the seemingly unlimited group of grass roots philosophers. You may have seen the signs or bumper stickers that say things like: "You're born, you get stuff and then you die, Live with it!" or "He who dies with the most stuff wins!"

Recently my sister's pet dog Levi died. She was dreading telling her grandchildren about this loss of part of their small world. When the grandkids came for a visit and she sat them down and explained it to them and got an unexpected response. Xavier who was about 2 years old at the time ran outside, looked up to the sky and yelled, "Hey God, how do you like your new dog?" Wow! It gives me goose bumps just thinking about what it means to have "a childlike faith" like that. This little fellow didn't waste anytime sorrowing, crying or worrying. He just accepted that God takes care of us after death and then went on with his normal happy routine of life.

I don't know about you, but the next time I face death, I'm praying for the faith that will allow me to say, "Hey God, how do you like your new child being with you?" Whether it's a husband, wife, child, father, mother, sister or brother if we are Christians then we are all children of God. Of course many like to believe there is a special place for dogs in heaven also… (*From Stories to Touch the Heart by Russ Lawson*).

Chewy… #2

HOW DID WE COPE

We really didn't know how to cope with this loss. What's the old question, "***How do you heal a broken heart***", that was where we were at this point. We intellectually understood all about the hurt and we could rationalize our loss, but none the less it still hurt and we still felt a very real loss in our lives.

We talked about getting another dog, but I was against it for a good while. Our lives were so busy, we had so many obligations; how could we take on another dog with our schedules and lifestyle. Then there was the reality of eventually having to face the loss of another pet we had come to love.

Of course I had my work to keep me busy and out of the house much of the time, while my wife was often there alone. I watched as she grieved for our little Ching for about 6 months and finally agreed to just "look around" and see what was available. What we found was it had now become much harder to find that same breed of dog, but that was what we wanted so we kept looking. Our little Ching had been so smart, so lovable, and so personable we just couldn't consider another breed.

After a couple of months of searching I ran across a Newspaper advertisement, (I tracked it down on the Internet), for Peek-a-Poo puppies. The problem was that it was in a different state about a 4 hour drive from us, but my wife made the call to the breeder and found out they had the runt of the litter available, a female, whose markings were almost identical to our first dog Ching.

We made the arrangement, made the trip and came home with the cutest little ball of fur you could ever imagine. She climbed up behind my wife's neck and seemed to love looking out the window and that remained her favorite place to ride the whole time she was part of our family. We named her Chewy, because she reminded us of a Star Wars Wookie, (and the fact that she liked to chew of things, but that's part of being a puppy). To say the least we fell in love with her very quickly. We skipped the box this time and just put her on the end of the bed where she seemed content to stay every night for the rest of her life.

You see, we had found that you fill a dog sized hole in your heart with another source of love; for us it became a 7 pound bundle of love called Chewy.

While Chewy was different from Ching in many ways, she was also the same in many ways. She had a wonderful personality; she loved people in general and seemed to always be filled with joy whenever she was around us. She was almost as smart as Ching also, though she may not have understood quite as many words, but she was smart none the less. Where Ching would respond almost immediately to whatever you said, Chewy would sometimes cock her head and look at you like she was processing what you had just said before responding. I understood that problem. When we were learning other languages while living in Africa I sometimes would have to stop and process what I had heard to translate it into terms to which I could respond. I don't know if that is what was happening with her, but she responded none the less.

Chewy joined our family not long after our first grandson was born so they grew up together in lots of ways. We often kept the grandson and he and Chewy would play together for hours. There were a couple incidents about which I wrote short articles which are found in my book, **"*Stories to touch the heart*"**. They give some insight into how she became part of our family.

SOMETIMES I SURPRISE EVEN ME!

Do you ever think about the things you do and just shake your head in wonder? I don't know if it goes with getting older or what, but it seems like I surprise myself more and more as time goes by. I do some things now that I would have never thought of doing years ago. No! I don't think my mind is going, but it may be that my priorities have changed or I have a new sense of what is important.

For example: This past week we noticed a swollen place on the tail of our little seven-month-old puppy, Chewy (care to guess why she has that name?). Anyway, after some discussion we decided to take her to the Vet and get it checked out. The Vet said he thought it was broken and wanted to X-ray the tail, we said yes. They did, it was and now she is on pain and anti-inflammation medication. How it happened we don't know, but that's not the point here. The point is that in times past we wouldn't have taken a dog to the Vet for a bump on her tail and wouldn't have even considered an X-ray (we could hardly afford X-rays for ourselves), after all she is just a dog!

Why did we do this now? What has made the change? I am sometimes amazed at myself and the things I do. I kind of scratch my head and say, "what's changed?" She's still just a dog isn't she? But, as I said earlier my priorities have changed or I have a new sense of what is important, a new perspective.

What's the point of this? People who don't love a dog can't fathom our caring for a dog in this way… It's the same way with people who don't have Jesus in their lives or don't love him that much! They can't fathom our lives, our priorities our sense of what is important. Why do we do the things we do… make the decisions we make? You see, the world in general doesn't have our perspective on life and they never will unless you explain it to them (which is what our life is suppose to be about anyway isn't it?).

So what has changed? I have and we all must! Our relationship to God must change to the point where we do things that the world just doesn't understand, because we have a new sense of what is really important. Stop saying we love God or love others, but show it in our life and actions. Perhaps when you learn to let the love of a dog into your life your heart begins to change towards people also. Sometimes you may surprise yourself with you perspective on things and towards people. When this happens perhaps you too can scratch your head and say, "Sometimes I amaze even me…" (*From Stories to Touch the Heart, by Russ Lawson*).

As our life continued to morph into something new on a daily basis we continued to grow in our relationship to our new puppy also. Following is a little piece I wrote for the Newspaper called **"She did it… Christopher and the dog"**.

SHE DID IT …. Christopher and the Dog…

"Our little grandson, Christopher is about 15 months old now, while we have a little five-pound puppy, Chewy who is 6 months old. To say the least they are just the right ages for each other. They love to play with each other and can literally entertain each other for hours. Christopher is not yet talking, but he does jabber quite a bit and says all of the important words, like Grandma and Grandpa, drink, ball, Mommy and Daddy.

Last night we were babysitting and Christopher and Chewy were having a great time. Christopher has learned that if he throws a ball Chewy will run and get it and bring it back to him. They were literally running one another ragged chasing that ball. At one point Christopher threw the ball and it went under the baby gate in the hall so the dog couldn't get it. They both ran over and were fussing about the ball that neither one of them could reach. I of course was watching all of this and said in my best grandpa voice, "What did you guys do now?" Quick as a wink Christopher turned and pointed to the dog, obviously saying, "It wasn't me, she did it." Of course grandma Melody and I got a good belly laugh out of that and told him, "No, the dog didn't do it, Christopher threw the ball."

This morning as I started thinking about that incident I realized how much that baby boy is just like us, supposed grown ups. When something goes wrong, when some problem arises far too often we are quick to point our finger to someone or something else as the cause. Back in the 1960's the comedian; Flip Wilson made famous the saying, *"The devil made me do it."* Whenever he did or said something bad, off color, something that shouldn't have been done or said, he would say, "the devil made me do it," as if this was suppose to make it all better. It was a way of shifting the blame to someone else for his mistakes.

I believe that is one of the greatest problems with our society today, many people do not want to take responsibility for their problems or the problems they cause others. We like to say, "Well he made me do it," "I only did it because they…"

The next time you are tempted to point you finger at someone else for your problems, as the old saying goes, "remember you have three fingers pointing back at you." Take responsibility for your life and your sin, don't blame, society, your boss, others … after all you are not 15 months old any longer… are you.

May God give us the ability to trust him enough that we can confess our wrongs, knowing he will understand and forgive." (*From Stories to Touch the Heart, by Russ Lawson*).

THE INFLUENCE OF PETS EVEN TO THE END

Yes, our "pet" Chewy had an extreme influence upon our lives and she was with us for about 15 years before falling prey to "old age". She hadn't been as perky as she had been for awhile and one day she seemed to be having a particular bad day. My wife took her to the Vet and the diagnosis was that she had congestive heart failure. The Vet gave her some water pills and told my wife to watch her. She took her home and she passed away about an hour later. Our oldest son came over just after that and checked on Chewy for my wife and confirmed that she had passed. He offered her the comfort and compassion that I could not until I got home from work.

Again, we held each other and cried for our furry child and grieved with broken hearts. Again we buried a piece of our hearts with that little fur covered body.

So once again we struggled with the question of how do we fill this hole in our heart, how do we stop the pain? We had the same concerns as when we had lost Ching our first fur baby. Our lives are busy, we are gone a lot. I not only worked during the week, but had a second job on the weekends preaching for a small country church. How do we overcome the problems associated with having another furry member to our family? How do we fill this ache, this hole in our heart under these circumstances? We knew the answer, but still we struggled for a number of reasons. We are older now; we have had dogs in our lives for almost 32 years and wondered how we would be able to care for another one in the future. However we knew that our hearts longed to have that hole filled with the unrestricted, sometimes undeserved love that only a pet can give.

Who Rescued Who?

A NEW APPROACH TO FINDING A DOG TO FILL THE HOLE...

We began looking around for another Peek-a-Poo to replace our beloved Chewy, but found that the "Mixed Breed" dogs of our past were now called, "Designer Dogs", and demanded far more money to pay for them. We realized that we could never hope to come up with the money to buy a puppy of this breed, even if she were going to be a family member.

We began looking around at adoption sites and local pounds as far away as 500 miles from home. We never found one Peek-a-poo, but did find lots of other small dogs who needed a home. After a couple of weeks we spotted a dog online that touched our hearts, it was a little Shih Tzu dog which had been abandoned, found wandering on the streets.

You have seen the pictures of dogs like her on television, pictures of the neglected dogs, long unkempt fur, malnourished, ribs and hip bones showing through her skin. At the first look on the internet we said, "***We not only need her, she needs us!***" It took a couple of weeks to get her processed and allow time for her previous owners to claim her if they chose to, but finally she was put up for adoption and my wife was there to "rescue" her.

Cassie #3 our rescue dog

We finally settled on the name "Cassie Valentine" for her, though she had no idea what that meant at the time. We got her on Valentines Day so I told my wife she was her Valentine's present.

She had gained a little weight and they had a vet check her out at the local pound, (we had been looking all over the country and found her less than 3 miles from our house). The pound was only going to keep her for a few days before putting her down; they said her age and condition would make it hard for them to find her a home. They estimated that she is around 12 years old, but we figured that we are older (more mature), also and would be able to relate better to her, so didn't think twice about rescuing her.

We immediately bathed her and took her to a local vet to give her a through exam, shots, etc. The vet also thought she is probably around 12 year old, and found she had 'Kennel cough', and was at least partially deaf. We and the Vet surmised after having her in our home for a week and seeing how she related to us, that she could have been a kennel kept dog, possible a breeder dog. The Vet said that it is not unusual for people to just put the dogs out on the street after they have been used up.

We also found that she also had no idea how to respond to us, most likely because she had very little human contact, at least loving human contact. It surprised us that she had no idea of how to play. We tried playing with her and just stared at us. We tried giving her toys, throwing balls, etc. and again she just stared at us. She had no idea of how to relate to humans who want to love her.

She was with us for about 4 years and even after all that time was somewhat slow to show a lot of affection; however she did decide that she liked her ears scratch or just to be petted sometimes and she eventually followed my wife everywhere. If my wife left the room, Cassie searched the house until she found her. She even allows me to hold her and pet her for short periods time, whereas before she wanted off of my lap after about a minute.

One of the good things is that she was very easy to train to go outside and potty, however she always stops and looks back to make sure we were still at the door. We have wondered if someone put her out and never let her back in…. She gained weight, from 8 pounds when we got her with skin hanging in folds to a healthy 12 pounds now. She was not fat, but she is filled out.

Cassie was a completely different dog from our first two dogs. It had taken months of love to get her to learn that some people can be nice. She never did learn to play and we noticed where our other dogs ran while Cassie jumped or bounded.

Eventually after she had been part of our family for awhile when we came home after having gone to the store or wherever she often just bounded, (bounced, around the house and ran back and forth between my wife and I like we are the greatest people in the world.

Cassie was also content we believe, often she would lie in her bed or on the carpet rolling around on her back acting like she is so happy. And talk about being happy and showing it… we give her some canned meat food every evening, (She had only a few teeth and ate the soft food better). She of course knew what time was suppose to be served and waits impatiently until we give it to her. After she ate her food she again rolled around of the floor and liked to root around under her bed acting like it is the best time of her life! It's the closest thing she does to playing up to this point. We smiled and laughed at her and told her what a pretty girl she was. She was our little rescue dog, but she rescued us also, filling that dog size hole in our hearts. That is what it is all supposed to be about anyway… isn't it?

We knew we wouldn't have her with us as long as our other furry children, but that's OK, we wanted to make her time with us a special and as happy as we could, because she also brought us joy. Would it be hard on us when she passes? Absolutely, but until that time we were be blessed and tried to be a blessing to her little furry life also.

After having her with us for about 4 years her heart began to give out. The Vet gave her medicine for that, but it never seemed like it helped that much. In the end the Vet told us that she thought it was time to let her go. She was suffering with several problems besides congestive heart failure. Again it took us a couple of weeks to process that information and make a decision, but we finally did. Again I held her and tried to comfort her until she drew her last breath.

MORE INSIGHT

The following is a Newspaper column I wrote about our new dog, perhaps something to consider as you try to fill the dog size hole in your heart.

———————————————————

OLD AND UNWANTED
By Russ Lawson

I'm getting to the age where many of the "young" people refer to me as "old". That's OK with me, I really don't care, I figure that the gray hair is a mark of the many adventures we have had in this life. The problem with getting older is that your body can no longer keep up with what your mind thinks it can do!

I'm much luckier than many people in this world, because even though I am "more mature" in age, I am also loved by those important to me. Now the reason I am thinking about this is because our family status just changed. You see, about 8 months ago our little "furry kid", (our dog), who had been with us for almost 16 years died. After struggling with the decision we went to the local Animal Shelter and found a little dog and rescued her.

Now what makes her special is that she was picked up as a stray and no one came to claim her. She was scruffy or scraggly looking with matted hair and quite a bit undernourished (you can easily feel her bones through her skin). The Shelter staff estimate her age to be about 12 year old, which makes it harder to find folks who are willing to adopt her. She was in the "OAU" category (old and unwanted). You see everyone wants a cute little puppy, but an older dog with just a few years left is another story. The bottom line was that if the Shelter didn't find someone to adopt her they would euthanize (or kill) her.

From the first time I saw her picture (scruffiness and all) I wanted her. I saw a scared little dog who didn't understand what was happening and was completely at the mercy of people. Being older ourselves and having had two small dogs in the past that lived to be near 16 we understand somewhat the limitations of age. We wanted to love her and give her the best (last) years that we can. We called everyday until they put her up for adoption because we surely didn't want the alternative to happen. That morning my wife was there when the doors opened, and now she is ours.

It seems that our society has also lost some very important values and one of them is honoring older folks. Our younger generation for the most part worships youth and rejects the concept that those who are older just might have something important to contribute, something as important as love and acceptance. Our "old dog," is already finding her way into our hearts. She was so over joyed to come home with us that she runs around like a puppy and climbs in our laps and cuddles up and exudes love, just for a few minutes at a time. My wife said it seemed a little strange that she should adapt so quickly. I replied, "Maybe she knows the fate that awaited her before we came along," probably not, but we knew and we acted because of what we knew.

Now looking at the spiritual application a bunch of scripture comes to mind as it relates to this. The scriptures tell us, *"While we were still sinners Christ died for us"* and that *"he was not willing that any of us should perish but all come to salvation"*. You see, we may be older, we may be a bit scruffy looking too, but not to God. God understood the fate that awaits those, who like that little dog, lost and alone in a big world will suffer. He determined that he would go to any extreme to rescue us and he did. He died for us that we can live eternally in the arms of a loving master. Are you there yet?

A FOLLOW UP NEWSPAPER ARTICLE:

THE GIFT
By Russ Lawson

I've written a couple of times about our new rescued dog, Cassie, but something I don't think I have mentioned is that she was a gift to my wife. Our little dog Chewy died this past summer and my wife has been grieving every since. Actually, until we got our new furry kid I didn't realize how much I missed her too. Anyway, the search for a new dog began as a search for a special dog for my wife for Valentines Day. We got her a few days late, but the name which was chosen for her is "Cassie Valentine".

You probably have heard the saying which goes, "it's the gift that keeps on giving," well that's Cassie. She has bonded with both of us, but especially my wife as she is with her so much more. My wife can't leave the room without a little black shadow following her. She gets so excited when we give her canned dog food that she prances around, rolls on her back and wags all over, (the dog, not my wife). She returns the blessing of love, maybe because she understands the gift she has been given and remembers what it was like not to have those who loved her and cared for her.

Our granddaughter has also received a gift through this little fur ball. She has "suggested" for the past six months that "you guys REALLY need a new dog". What she was really saying is that she wanted us to get a dog that she could play with. However, blessings sometimes bless us in unexpected ways. Our 9 year old granddaughter has begun hand sewing clothes for the dog. She has made her a coat and Shaw and a neckerchief. They really look cute and she is proud of her ability to make these little gifts for the dog. Gifts can be blessings, which fill our needs, give us something we can't give ourselves, or even that which causes us to share with others.

From another aspect though, we understand that this gift comes with responsibility. Dogs take care; they take time, and there is some expense with having a dog. That's not unlike the gift of being a Christian is it? Someone reminded me again the other day that Dog spelled backwards is GOD, maybe that's not an accident that it's that way.

I like this modern translation of **Ephesians 2:8** that tells us, *"**God saved you by his grace when you believed. And you can't take credit for this; it is a gift from God**."* Often in the New Testament we read of the reaction of those who come into contact with Jesus. They rejoiced, gave thanks and went and told others what Jesus has done for them, because the gift he has given them.

How are you doing with that? In **Matthew 28:119-20** we read of Jesus saying, *"**Therefore go and make disciples of all nations, baptizing them in the name of the Father and of the Son and of the Holy Spirit, and teaching them to obey everything I have commanded you. And surely I am with you always, to the very end of the age**."* You see, this is our response to the gift! It is the gift that keeps on giving and one for which we must keep on rejoicing.

Is another dog in the picture?

After about 9 months we finally decided that we needed a new fur baby in our lives. At this point we have begun searching for the new member of the family to adopt or rescue. We know our limitations and have had almost 40 years of experience with the joy, love and pain of having a fur baby. We haven't found her yet, but are sure there is a little dog out there somewhere waiting for us.

HOW OTHERS DEAL WITH THE LOSS OF THEIR DOGS

One of the things I had hoped to do when I started writing this short book is to talk with others who have lost dogs and find how they have dealt with the loss. So below I have added the stories of some friends who have lost their furry family members. Perhaps they will help each of us understand that we are not alone with how we feel about our furry children and how we suffer when we loose them.

GRACE'S STORY

We got Rocky as a pup & he basically was with us as our girls went from Young Girls to Young Grown up Ladies. He was a constant in our lives & he always made me feel so very special & loved. And it was never about him; he was a selfless little dog with a tremendous personality & and the cutest puppy face ever (even at 15 years old in human years!).

When my both girls left the nest & married, he stuck by me Night & Day ... always greeting me with a wagging tail & lots of kisses.... and oh, how very much I miss him!!!

It's been a little over one year now since I lost ROCKY & I really cannot say that it gets easier, in fact, at times the pain feels unbearable but I do thank God for all those years that I did have him as my Faithful Friend & I do plead with the Good Lord to reunite us One Fine Day in Heaven! That is the only way I can cope, believing that someday we will be together again!

I also had a Cuddle Clone stuffed toy custom made to his liking which I keep in my living room. And while this might sound silly to some, it really does comfort me as I stroke it & whisper a prayer hoping that he is happy & restored to good health & is with God now! Do I ever doubt this? Yes, at times I do but then I quickly & fervently ask God to increase my Faith and to help me through until I see his little tail wagging and feel his sweet kisses on my face!

I love you, Rocky! Thanks for teaching me how to give generously and to love deeply.
Rocky will forever be in My Heart!

Betty's Story

Betty

Jojo was given to me by my husband for a wedding anniversary present. What a surprise. That beautiful little blonde ball fur that just ran all over and licked and kissed me and I immediately fell in love.

Jojo became an intimate part of our life. She traveled with us slept with us played with us helped us raise our kids. But after 16 years her health began to fail. We of course visited the vet regularly and the vet told us finally that it was time to think about letting her go. She had arthritis and a couple of tumors. She was obviously in pain and there was nothing that we did could make it better.

We prayed about it and finally made the decision that it was time to let her go home. I don't know when we'll ever find another love as deep as that one that was uncompromising one that was unfaltering one that loved us even when we sometimes were not lovable.

We grieved so hard it was just like losing a child she was truly our fur baby and will never forget her. Right now we're hurting too much to think about getting another dog but we may to share in that joy and perhaps even to rescue some pup who's been rejected.

THOUGHTS ON GRIEVING...

In reality, grieving for your dog is not much different than grieving for the loss of a human friend or family member. Some folks go through more steps than others in the grieving process, but there are at least two that are basic that each of have to go through.

First...Grieve!

The first thing you need to do is to admit you have deep feelings for the one you just lost and let yourself experience the grieving process. One of the problems with the loss of a pet is that those who don't have pets or don't have a loving relationship with their pets honestly don't understand what you are going through. Because it is that we are tempted to hide our grief, tears and sorrow, especially when they make comments like, "it was just a dog."

Don't be afraid to cry at the loss! With each of our dog's deaths we had a "mini wake" if you will. Our youngest son came over and cried with us and we had a burial service, even had prayer thanking God for blessing us with that bundle of joy and asking to help us recover from the loss.

Second... Try and adjust to the loss but don't deny it happened!

When a human loved one dies we understand when we start to pick up the phone to call them or think about them on their birthdays or holidays. Do you really expect it to be any different with the loss or your furry family member? Don't hide the pictures, don't apologize when you find yourself looking for them and turn around and they are not there.

We need to remember those we love when they pass, whether furry or not. It might be painful to remember those things, but it is not a sign of weakness, it is a sign of love, it is a demonstration of our character, or what makes us who we are. If someone looks at us funny when we suddenly break out in tears or call a name of a pet that is no longer with us, that's fine, it's our grief not theirs. We don't have to please them; we have to honor the memory of the one we love in our own way.

I read a quote today that said basically, "*They say that time makes the loss less painful, but that's not true, it just gives us more time to learn how to deal with the loss*." Just as when dealing with the loss of a human, the pain of the loss of our pet lessens, but it never really goes away.

Third, realize that lots of folks just won't understand.

Dog owners or dog lovers have a special relationship to their furry family as well as to other dog lovers. At my place of work I have learned of many who have furry family members and it is a point of contact for us. Often we will greet each other and ask about family, but more often about our furry family members. I've noticed as we talk about our furry kids there are sometimes some who just look at us as if we are crazy. They have no idea why this is so important to us or why a dog takes such precedence in our lives. So, realize that there are lots of folks who just won't understand why you are grieving. That's OK though, each of us are different in our loves and what makes us happy and fills the hole that sometimes needs filled in our hearts. Don't let the lack of understanding of some people hurt your hearts further; give yourself permission to grieve as long as you need to.

Fourth, when possible acknowledge others when they face the loss of their loved one!

With the loss of both of our dogs we actually received sympathy cards from several friends who understood our loss. Those meant more to us than many folks can imagine. The idea that there were some who understood what that loss meant to us was a tremendous encouragement. Quite honestly we look at those folks with a special love for their sharing in our sorrow and loss.

Concluding thoughts

Owning a dog, (hopefully making them part of your family), is not a decision to be taken lightly. It is a big responsibility if it is done right. We all have seen the pictures on the television of neglected and abused dogs and I'm sure you don't want to be part of that group.

When you make a dog into a fur baby or an intimate part of your family it demands time and resources. Not just food, but time, lots of time and financial resources also. There will be Veterinarian bills just like you have to take your children to the doctor from time to time. If you don't have the time or the resources, please don't take on the responsibly for a pet.

Pets trust you and rely on you for their every need and that is a lot of responsibility. We have often said that having a dog is like having a toddler, they really demand that much care.

But having said that, I also want to say they are such a blessing that once you have had a real "fur baby", you won't want to be without one. Are they worth the trouble, the worry and expense? Yes they are. Take it from someone who has been there and had fur babies for the past 38 years.

So when it is time for them to pass from your life, grieve, but remember the good times and how they made you the number one most important thing in their lives. Rescue or adopt another if you can and you will be blessed and the grief will find relief.